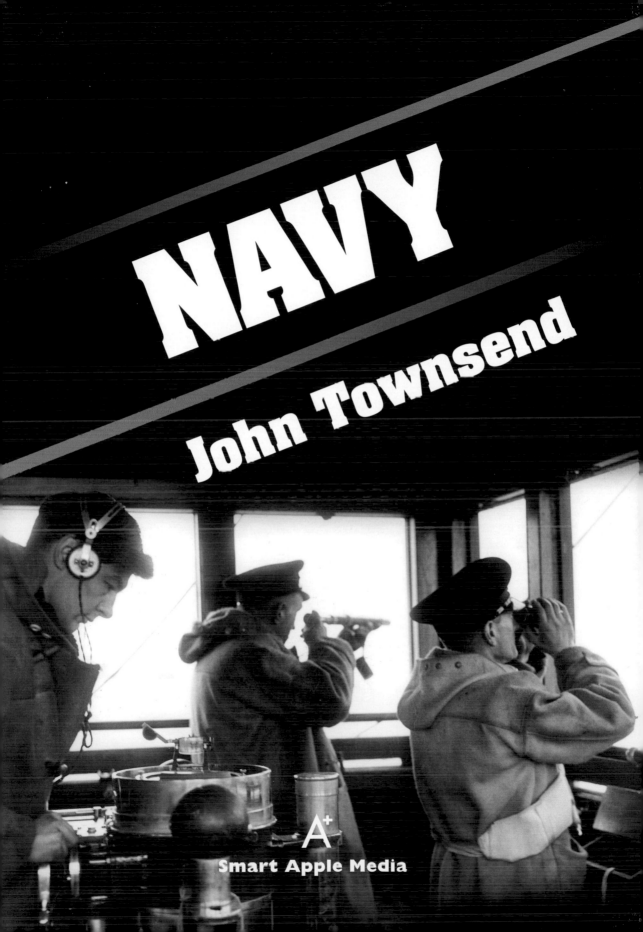

NAVY

John Townsend

Smart Apple Media

Published by Smart Apple Media, an imprint of Black Rabbit Books
P.O. Box 3263, Mankato, Minnesota 56002
www.smartapplemedia.com

Published by arrangement with Watts Publishing, London.

Cataloging-in-Publication Data is available from the Library of Congress
ISBN: 978-1-59920-984-5   (library binding)
ISBN: 978-1-68071-002-1   (eBook)

Picture credits:
Bettmann/Corbis: front cover.
DEA/De Agostini/Getty Images: 5.
GeoEye: 20.
The Granger Collection/Topfoto: 17.
Hulton Archive/Getty Images: 7.
MPI/Getty Images 29.
National Archive/HIP/Topfoto: 4.
Picturepoint/Topham: 9, 27t.
Popperfoto/Getty Images: 11, 13.
2nd Class William G Roy/US Navy: 21.
Topfoto: 1, 6, 8, 10, 27b.
ullsteinbild/Topfoto: 18, 28.
US Naval Historical Center: 16.
US Navy: 12, 19, 23, 24t, 24b, 26.
courtesy of ussubvetsofwwll.org: 22.
Wikipedia: 14, 25.

Every attempt has been made to clear copyright. Should there be any inadvertent omission please apply to the publisher for rectification.

Printed in the United States by CG Book Printers
North Mankato, Minnesota

PO 1727
3-2015

Contents

War at Sea

During the 1930s, Adolf Hitler and his Nazi Party became the ruling power in Germany. By 1939 it was clear that Germany planned to take over Europe. When German forces invaded Poland, Britain and France warned Hitler to stop. He refused and war was declared. Other countries soon became involved as World War II spread.

THE
BRITISH NAVY
guards the freedom of us all

This Royal Navy recruiting poster shows how important navies were during World War II.

During the six years of World War II, thousands of ships manned by millions of sailors formed a constantly alert action force on the oceans around the world. The many sea battles they fought had a major impact on the outcome of the war.

Each navy had two main tasks:
- Attack enemy targets (e.g. ships, ports, shore installations in other countries)
- Defend its own shores from attack, as well as protect sea lanes and friendly shipping. Also to ferry troops from place to place.

Sunk! A direct hit on an Allied warship sends it to the bottom of the sea.

AF FACTS

World War II lasted from 1939 to 1945 and involved 61 countries.

- 25 million people in all armed forces were killed; many more were injured.
- Allies: forces fighting against Germany and Japan, such as France, Britain, and the US.
- Axis: the armed forces of Germany, Japan, Italy, and others

ACTION STATS

Sizes of German, British, and French Navy Staffs in 1939

German navy	78,000
Royal Navy	120,000
French navy	160,000

Hitler's Navy

Hitler was commander-in-chief of the *Kriegsmarine* (the German navy) from 1935 to 1945. Although its navy was smaller than those of the *Allies*, Germany had plans for building a far superior naval force. "Plan Z" aimed to create a fleet of 800 ships manned by 200,000 men.

The Kriegsmarine's most lethal ships were its *U-boats* ("undersea boats," or submarines). For the first few years of the war, U-boats attacked Allied ships carrying supplies across the North Atlantic Ocean.

U-boats hunted in groups called "wolf packs," and fired *torpedoes* (underwater missiles). U-boats sank thousands of Allied ships during what became known as the Battle of the Atlantic. Allied navies had to find ways of striking back at U-boats.

The ensign (ship's flag) of the Kriegsmarine flying on a German U-boat.

German U-boats traveled on the surface before submerging to avoid detection and to attack.

ACTION STATS

At the beginning of World War II, the German navy had only 55 U-boats. During the war it built another 1,150. In the Battle of the Atlantic, U-boats sank over 2,600 ships, while the Allies sank almost 800 U-boats. Of the 40,000 men who served on U-boats during World War II, 30,000 never returned. This was the highest casualty rate of any armed service in the history of modern warfare.

AF FACTS

On September 3, 1939, a U-boat fired a torpedo and sank the British liner SS *Athenia* without warning and against the rules of war. Over 100 passengers were killed, but Hitler said the Kriegsmarine was not responsible.

The Royal Navy

During World War II, Britain imported about half its food and all its oil by sea. It needed a strong naval force to protect *merchant ships* transporting these vital supplies from North America and elsewhere. Much of the Royal Navy's efforts were directed toward protecting the critical North Atlantic sea routes from attack.

The Royal Navy used fast and agile escort vessels to attack U-boats.

ACTION STATS

At the start of World War II, the Royal Navy operated more ships than any other. By the end of the war, the US Navy had become the world's largest.

In 1939 the Royal Navy had 15 battleships, 7 aircraft carriers, 66 cruisers, 184 destroyers, 45 escort and patrol vessels, and 60 submarines. Many more of each type were completed during the war.

AF FACTS

Not all the Royal Navy's efforts were directed at U-boats. In May and June 1940 it provided critical cover when thousands of British and French troops had to be evacuated from Dunkirk in France.

Canada and the US helped the Royal Navy by providing escort vessels to protect convoys (groups) of merchant ships from the deadly U-boats. From August 1941, these ships used radar, which could detect a U-boat *periscope* at a range of 1.25 miles (2 km). In 1942 the U-boat *U-559* was captured with an "Enigma" coding machine and code books on board. This information helped the Allies track U-boats and attack them.

Nazi Germany invaded France in May 1940. A huge fleet of small civilian ships and Royal Navy vessels evacuated more than 300,000 Allied troops from Dunkirk, which was under attack from German aircraft.

Case Study: Battle of the River Plate

The Battle of the River Plate was the first major naval battle of World War II. Three of the Royal Navy's ships (HMS *Exeter, Ajax,* and *Achilles*) took on the mighty German *battleship Admiral Graf Spee,* which was sinking merchant ships off the coast of South America.

ACTION STATS

Admiral Graf Spee
- Weight: 14,890 tons (13,508 t)
- Length: 610 ft. (186 m)
- Max speed: 29.5 knots
- Armament: 6x11-in. (28 cm) guns, 8x5.9-in. (15 cm) guns, 6x4.1-in. (10.5 cm) guns, 4x.5-in. (3.7 cm) guns, 10x0.8-in. (2 cm) guns, 8x20.9-in. (53 cm) torpedo tubes, 2 aircraft

In December 1939, the four ships engaged in a famous battle in the River Plate estuary in South America. The massive guns of the *Graf Spee* scored hits on all three British ships. HMS *Exeter* was badly damaged. The Royal Navy's smaller guns failed to penetrate the *Graf Spee*'s 5.5-inch-thick (14 cm) thick steel armor, until finally a shell damaged the ship's fuel system.

Opposite: The Graf Spee *on fire and sinking after the battle.*

The *Graf Spee* limped into the *neutral* port of Montevideo, where the captain decided to destroy his ship rather than let the Allies seize it. The captain wrote a letter to Hitler, then killed himself. The end of the *Graf Spee* was celebrated by the Allies as their first real naval victory of the war.

AF FACTS

Germany reported that the *Graf Spee* had sunk an enemy ship and badly damaged two others, while only being lightly damaged herself. In fact, HMS *Exeter* was able to reach the Falkland Islands for repairs.

Light cruiser HMS Ajax, *which took part in the Battle of the River Plate.*

Battleships

Battleships were the largest and most powerful warships of each navy. They had the thickest armor and huge firepower from large-caliber guns. Battleships were the leading vessels of each naval fleet and rarely operated alone. They were protected by faster, smaller ships.

A group of US battleships, pictured in 1945 at the end of World War II.

When enemy fleets met, the battleships would form a "line of battle" and maneuver to maximize the number of guns that could fire.

After the destruction of the *Graf Spee*, the pride of the German navy was the *Tirpitz*, one of the most modern battleships of the war. With armor over 11.8 inches (30 cm) thick and massive firepower, this was a battleship the Allied navies had to take seriously. Eventually, in 1944, she was sunk by British aircraft. Huge aerial bombs exploded the battleship's own ammunition and she rolled over and sank, trapping more than 1,000 men inside.

This photo shows the Tirpitz *anchored in Nazi-occupied Norway. She was found and sunk by Royal Air Force bombers.*

ACTION STATS

Tirpitz

- **Weight: 42,900 tons (38,918 t)**
- **Length: 823 ft. (251 m)**
- **Max speed: 30 knots**
- **Range: 10,191 mi. (16,400 km) at 19 knots**
- **Armament: 8x15-in. (38 cm) guns, 12x5.9-in. (15 cm) guns, 16x4.1-in. (10.5 cm) AA (anti-aircraft) guns, 16x1.5-in. (3.7 cm) AA guns, 8x21-in. (53.3 cm) torpedo tubes, 4 aircraft**
- **Crew: 2,400**

Case Study: The *Bismarck*

 This painting shows the Bismarck *firing its main guns.*

The sinking of two great warships in 1941 brought an end to the age when battleships were the major forces in naval warfare. Submarines and aircraft carriers took over as the key vessels in the war at sea.

The sister ship of the *Tirpitz* was the *Bismarck*, one of Germany's most famous battleships of World War II. It was a mighty ship. The Royal Navy sent HMS *Hood*, its prize battleship, to attack it in the North Atlantic. *Bismarck* fired its massive guns, smashing a shell through *Hood*'s deck. A huge explosion tore the ship in half and it sank in minutes. All but three of the 1,419 crew members were lost.

ACTION STATS

Bismarck
Launched in 1939
Armament:
- 8x15-in. (38 cm) guns
- 12x5.9-in. (15 cm) guns
- 16x4.1-in. (10.5 cm) AA guns
- 16x1.5-in. (3.7 cm) AA guns
- 4 aircraft

HMS *Hood*
Launched in 1918
Armament (1941):
- 8x15-in. (38 cm) guns
- 14x4-in. (10 cm) guns
- 24x2-lb. (0.9 kg) guns
- 20x0.5-in. (1.3 cm) machine guns
- 4x21-in. (53.3 cm) torpedo tubes

After this disaster the Royal Navy sent a large force to attack the *Bismarck*. Heavy gunfire from battleships HMS *Rodney* and *King George V* hammered the *Bismarck* until it was ablaze. Finally, HMS *Dorsetshire* fired three torpedoes, and the *Bismarck* sank with the loss of more than 2,000 men.

AF FACTS

The Royal Navy was able to sink the *Bismarck* because the German battleship's rudder had been smashed by a torpedo fired by a plane from aircraft carrier HMS *Ark Royal*. The *Bismarck* was a sitting duck.

Battleship HMS Hood, *sunk by the* Bismarck *in 1941.*

Japan Attacks

In the 1930s, Japan built one of the world's largest navies. This enabled it to invade Malaya and the East Indies for their oil and rubber. However, Japan feared the US might try to stop its plans so it attacked the US Pacific Fleet.

The Japanese battleship Yamato, seen here in 1941, was the biggest and most heavily armed battleship ever built.

On December 7, 1941, the Japanese bombed the US naval base at Pearl Harbor in Hawaii. All the Imperial Japanese Navy's top aircraft carriers with their fleet of over 420 planes were used in the attack. More than 2,400 US personnel were killed and 21 US ships were sunk or damaged. Over 188 US aircraft were also destroyed.

ACTION STATS

When Japan entered World War II, the Imperial Japanese Navy had a formidable number of ships:

Battleships: 12
Aircraft carriers: 21
Light carriers: 4
Cruisers: 45
Destroyers: 141
Submarines: 171

Until the attack on Pearl Harbor, the US had not joined World War II, other than giving naval support to Allied merchant shipping. Suddenly the US was forced into the war and within days, other *Axis* nations declared war on the US. The Pacific Ocean was set to become a major arena for naval battles with the mighty Imperial Japanese Navy.

Battleship USS West Virginia *burned and sank after being hit with seven aerial torpedoes in the attack on Pearl Harbor.*

The US Navy

After the attack on Pearl Harbor, the US Navy had to recover quickly and engage in the war against Japanese expansion in the Pacific. Their first chance to fight back was in May 1942 at the Battle of the Coral Sea. This was the first naval battle where the enemies fired without their ships coming within sight of one another. Japan, until then seemingly unstoppable, had now been challenged.

ACTION STATS

The US Navy's aircraft carriers operated in the Pacific so that US planes could more easily attack Japanese forces. With 4,500 pilots and 3,400 planes, the US had more air power than the Japanese navy.

YOUR NAVY-FIRST LINE OF **ATTACK**

NAVY DAY OCT. 27TH

After the US entered the war, thousands of sailors were needed to man its ships. Posters like this one helped find recuits.

New ships had to be built fast, and the USA had the money and manpower to do just that. By 1945, hundreds of new US ships were in operation, including 18 new aircraft carriers and 8 new battleships—a total of 6,768 ships by the end of the war.

Four huge *Iowa*-class battleships were launched to defend the fleet and attack Japanese targets in the Pacific Ocean. USS *Iowa* had fearsome firepower, but one of its first missions was to take US President Franklin Roosevelt to an Allied conference in Casablanca, North Africa, in 1943.

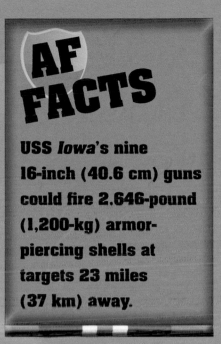

AF FACTS

USS *Iowa*'s nine 16-inch (40.6 cm) guns could fire 2,646-pound (1,200-kg) armor-piercing shells at targets 23 miles (37 km) away.

USS Iowa *remained a part of the US Navy until 1990. This photo shows the ship firing its huge guns during an exercise in 1984.*

Case Study: Battle of Midway

Six months after the attack on Pearl Harbor, the US Navy defeated Japan in one of the most important naval battles of World War II. The Battle of Midway in June 1942 crushed Japan's naval strength when four of its aircraft carriers were destroyed. The Imperial Japanese Navy never fully recovered from its defeat at Midway.

The US fleet had a naval base on the small Midway Islands in the North Pacific Ocean. The Japanese navy set out to ambush the fleet, then take over the base. US intelligence had already discovered this plan, so its ships were prepared and waiting.

The fierce battle that followed destroyed four of the Japanese navy's vital aircraft carriers but only one US aircraft carrier—USS *Yorktown*. Although the US base at Midway was damaged by an air attack, it remained operational and played a vital part in the US's eventual success in the Pacific.

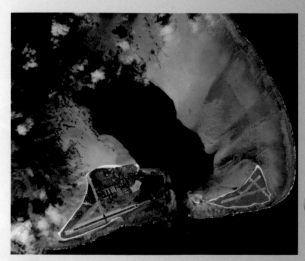

 This aerial photo of the Midway Islands shows the runways of the US base.

ACTION STATS

Casualties and Losses:

US
- 1 aircraft carrier
- 1 destroyer
- 150 aircraft
- 307 killed

Japan
- 4 aircraft carriers
- 1 cruiser
- 248 carrier aircraft
- 3,057 killed

AF FACTS

After it was hit several times and attempts at saving it had failed, the *Yorktown* finally capsized and sank on June 7, 1942. The wreck was found in 1998.

Smoke pours from USS Yorktown *after being hit by Japanese dive bombers at Midway.*

Subs in the Pacific

World War II submarines were surface ships that could travel underwater for only a short time. Diesel engines gave them a high speed and long range on the surface. However, speed and range were very limited below the surface. This was because the batteries that powered a sub underwater needed regular recharging by surfacing to run the air-breathing diesel engines.

ACTION STATS

USS *Balao*
- Weight: 1,550 tons (1,406 t)
- Length: 312 ft. (95 m)
- Max speed: 20 knots
- Max speed (submerged): under 9 knots
- Range: 12,427 mi. (20,000 km) at surface speed of 10 knots
- Armament: 1x4-in. (10 cm) deck gun, 1x1.6-in. (40 mm) AA gun, 10x21-in. (53.3 cm) torpedo tubes with 24 torpedoes
- Crew: 80

Balao could stay submerged for 48 hours.

USS Balao, pictured on the surface with some of its crew on deck.

Japanese midget submarines fill a Tokyo dockyard after the war.

Submarines formed less than 2 percent of the US Navy, but sank over 30 percent of Japan's navy, including eight aircraft carriers. US subs also crippled the Japanese economy by sinking almost five million tons of shipping—over 60 percent of Japan's merchant ships.

However, there was a high cost—314 submarines served with the US Navy in the war, most of these in the Pacific. Fifty-two US submarines never returned, nor did 3,505 sailors. This was the highest percentage of men killed in action of any US force in World War II.

AF FACTS

Midget submarines operated by a crew of one or two were used by navies in WWII. Japan also used suicide midget submarines as well as suicide scuba divers who would swim under boats with explosives on bamboo poles and destroy both the boat and themselves.

Aircraft Carriers

The success of aircraft carriers during World War II meant that many navies concentrated their efforts on building this important vessel.

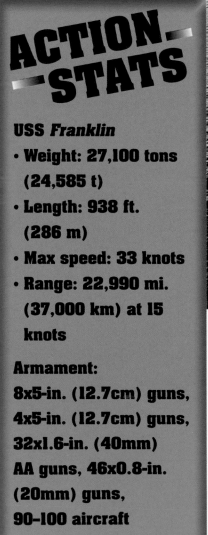

ACTION STATS

USS *Franklin*
- **Weight: 27,100 tons (24,585 t)**
- **Length: 938 ft. (286 m)**
- **Max speed: 33 knots**
- **Range: 22,990 mi. (37,000 km) at 15 knots**

Armament:
8x5-in. (12.7cm) guns, 4x5-in. (12.7cm) guns, 32x1.6-in. (40mm) AA guns, 46x0.8-in. (20mm) guns, 90–100 aircraft

The mighty Franklin *steaming in the Pacific, its flight deck crowded with aircraft.*

The wings of most carrier aircraft folded to save space. This is the USS Essex *pictured in March 1943.*

Japan's massive carrier Shinano *remains the largest ship ever sunk by a submarine.*

An aircraft carrier's main function was to act as a seagoing airbase. Each carrier had over 1,000 sailors and over 30 aircraft. The US Navy had more than 90 carriers during the war, Japan about 30, and the Royal Navy had 24.

The USS *Franklin*, nicknamed "Big Ben," was one of 24 *Essex*-class aircraft carriers built during World War II as the backbone of the US Navy's combat fleet. Entering service in 1944, it served in campaigns in the Pacific. The ship was badly damaged by a Japanese air attack in March 1945, with the loss of over 800 of its crew. USS *Franklin* was the most heavily damaged US carrier to survive the war.

AF FACTS

Apart from being the largest carrier built at the time, the Imperial Japanese Navy's *Shinano* (above) was the shortest-lived carrier in World War II. On its maiden voyage in November 1944, it was torpedoed by the USS *Archer-Fish* submarine. It kept sailing but lost power and, after 11 hours, the huge ship capsized with all its 1,350 crew.

Destroyers

When torpedoes were developed in the late 1800s, navies realized they needed small, fast warships to protect their fleets. These "torpedo-boat *destroyers*" were smaller than cruisers and, by World War II, had become known simply as "destroyers."

ACTION STATS

The US Navy had 100 new destroyers when it entered the war in 1941. The following year, the first of a new batch of 175 destroyers (the *Fletcher* class) went into action in the Pacific.

USS McGowan *was a destroyer. It was launched in 1943 and saw extensive service during World War II and afterward.*

This picture shows a torpedo being launched from a ship.

Destroyers became essential for attacking torpedo-firing submarines and preventing them from getting in range to attack *cruisers*, battleships, or aircraft carriers. They also had to prevent enemy destroyers closing in to strike with torpedoes, and scouting waters for submarines or mines, often close to shore.

Many ships were badly damaged after hitting enemy mines (floating bombs) in the sea. Some mines were dropped by aircraft. Others were anchored unseen just below the surface. Navies also used destroyers to drag a device that sliced through the mines' mooring lines. The mine would float to the surface where it could be shot at and safely exploded. Another method used electrical cables to pass pulses of electricity through the water to blow up the mines.

A direct hit explodes a floating mine, protecting other ships from danger.

Final Naval Battles

Battles in the Pacific Ocean continued to the very end of World War II. As the war in Europe was coming to an end, the US was preparing for a major sea battle to win the war against Japan. This turned out to be one of the biggest naval conflicts of all, with huge losses of life.

A Japanese kamikaze suicide pilot crashes his bomb-laden plane into a US ship during the final stages of the war in the Pacific.

The battle for the island of Okinawa, to the south of Japan, in April 1945, was a bloodbath. More than 7,000 US *personnel* were killed on land and 5,000 were lost at sea. More than 32,000 were wounded. The Japanese lost 107,000 men and 7,400 were taken prisoner. Although 16 Japanese ships were sunk compared to 36 US ships, Japan lost 4,000 aircraft as well as its most powerful battleship, the *Yamato*. Nearly all its sailors were killed.

The last Allied ship sunk by enemy action in World War II was the submarine USS *Bullhead*. This was on August 6, 1945, the day the US attacked the Japanese city of Hiroshima with the first atomic bomb. Eight days later World War II was over.

Japanese officials sign the treaty of surrender aboard USS Missouri *on September 2, 1945.*

AF FACTS

In Europe, Allied troops finally closed in on Berlin in April 1945 and the Nazis were defeated. Hitler killed himself and Germany surrendered. VE (Victory in Europe) Day was celebrated on May 8, 1945. Japan finally surrendered three months later, on August 14, 1945.

World War II Timeline

Some of the key naval events of World War II

1939 September 1: World War II begins
September–onward: Battle of the Atlantic
December: Battle of the River Plate

1940 May 25–June 4: Evacuation of forces from Dunkirk
November: Battle of Taranto in the Mediterranean

1941 May: Sinking of HMS *Hood* and *Bismarck*
December 7: Japanese attack US at Pearl Harbor

1942 May: Battle of the Coral Sea
June: Battle of Midway
October: *U-559* sunk; German Enigma machine and
naval codebooks captured

1943 September: Operation Jaywick
December: Battle of the North Cape

1944 June 6: D-Day — Invasion of Nazi-occupied France
by Allied forces
June: Battle of the Philippine Sea
August: German battleship *Tirpitz* sunk

1945 March-June: Battle of Okinawa
August 14: Japan surrenders; World War II ends

Glossary

AA guns — anti-aircraft guns

Allies — countries (US, Britain and its Empire, Soviet Union) opposing the Axis forces

Axis — countries (Germany, Italy, Japan) opposing the Allies

battleship — the biggest warships of World War II, with the largest and heaviest guns

caliber — the diameter of a gun barrel and the shell it fires. German naval guns were described in metric measurements (eg. 38 cm); British and US guns were described in Imperial measurements (eg. 15 in)

cruisers — large, fast warships smaller than battleships but larger than destroyers

destroyers — fast warships smaller than cruisers and armed with torpedos; used for anti-submarine and escort duties

knot — one nautical mile per hour (1.85 kilometres or 1.15 miles)

Kriegsmarine — the navy of Nazi Germany in World War II

maiden voyage — very first journey or mission

merchant ships — any ships carrying civilian supplies and armed only for self-defense

mine — anti-ship bombs that float just under the surface and explode on contact

neutral — not joining either side in a conflict

periscope — an instrument that allows crew members in a submarine to see above the surface of the water

personnel — people employed for a task, such as in the navy

torpedoes — underwater missiles launched by a submarine or a destroyer

U-boat — German submarine

Index